LITTLE KIDS
FIRST
BIG
BOOK OF
THINGS
THAT GO

Karen de Seve

NATIONAL GEOGRAPHIC KIDS

WASHINGTON, D.C.

CONTENTS

INTRODUCTION

If you like things that go, you have come to the right place! Each chapter in this book explores a different type of vehicle, those from the early days up to spacecraft, and ends with a fun game to reinforce the ideas that were covered. Throughout the book are examples of inventions that have improved how we've gotten around since people first had a need to go from one place to another.

CHAPTER ONE introduces the notion of things that go, from people to animals to sleds. Engaging images and callouts invite readers to think about how they get around.

CHAPTER TWO describes how the invention of wheels changed the way humans get around.

CHAPTER THREE explores getting around without the help of horses and other animals that powered vehicles. Electricity and steam were the main sources of power, and they are still used today.

CHAPTER FOUR investigates vehicles that burn gasoline to go. Most of today's vehicles are powered this way.

CHAPTER FIVE features some of the biggest things that go on land and sea.

CHAPTER SIX takes the reader airborne, from the earliest days of human flight to space exploration.

HOW TO USE THIS BOOK

COLORFUL PHOTOGRAPHS illustrate each spread, supporting the text and showcasing different types of vehicles from around the world.

POP-UP FACTS sprinkled throughout the book provide added information about things that go.

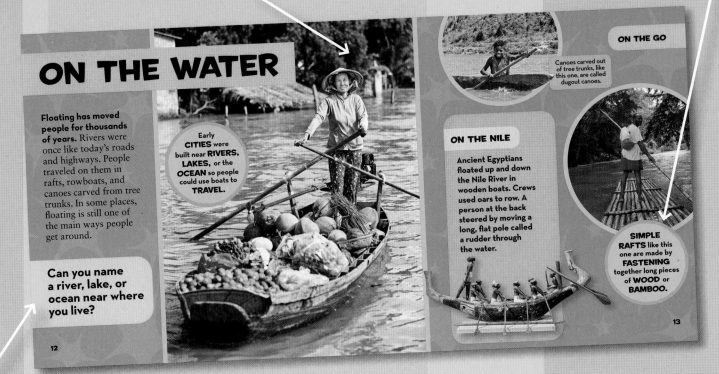

ON THE WATER

Floating has moved people for thousands of years. Rivers were once like today's roads and highways. People traveled on them in rafts, rowboats, and canoes carved from tree trunks. In some places, floating is still one of the main ways people get around.

Can you name a river, lake, or ocean near where you live?

Early **CITIES** were built near **RIVERS, LAKES,** or the **OCEAN** so people could use boats to **TRAVEL.**

12

ON THE GO

Canoes carved out of tree trunks, like this one, are called dugout canoes.

ON THE NILE

Ancient Egyptians floated up and down the Nile River in wooden boats. Crews used oars to row. A person at the back steered by moving a long, flat pole called a rudder through the water.

SIMPLE RAFTS like this one are made by **FASTENING** together long pieces of **WOOD** or **BAMBOO.**

13

INTERACTIVE QUESTIONS in each section encourage conversations related to the topic.

PARENT TIPS in the back of the book provide fun activity suggestions that relate to things that go.

A **GAME** at the end of each chapter reinforces concepts covered in that section.

A **GLOSSARY** in the final pages provides definitions for key terms found throughout the text.

CHAPTER 1
ON THE GO

Let's go! In this chapter, you will learn about some of the first ways people traveled from place to place.

ACROSS THE LAND

WALKING is the **OLDEST WAY** to travel. It's still one of the **BEST WAYS** to get to many **PLACES.**

As soon as babies can crawl, they are on the go. Then comes walking and running. People all over the world still walk to get from one place to another.

Animals sometimes do the walking for us. People ride horses, donkeys, and camels.

READY, SET, GO! If you want to get somewhere **FAST** on your own **TWO FEET,** then **RUNNING** is the way to go.

What are some places you walk to from your home?

11

ON THE WATER

Floating has moved people for thousands of years. Rivers were once like today's roads and highways. People traveled on them in rafts, rowboats, and canoes carved from tree trunks. In some places, floating is still one of the main ways people get around.

Can you name a river, lake, or ocean near where you live?

Early **CITIES** were built near **RIVERS, LAKES,** or the **OCEAN** so people could use boats to **TRAVEL.**

Canoes carved out of tree trunks, like this one, are called dugout canoes.

ON THE NILE

Ancient Egyptians floated up and down the Nile River in wooden boats. Crews used oars to row. A person at the back steered by moving a long, flat pole called a rudder through the water.

SIMPLE RAFTS like this one are made by **FASTENING** together long pieces of **WOOD** or **BAMBOO**.

13

PADDLE AWAY!

This **KAYAK** has a **SMALL OPENING** in the center for a person to **SIT.**

A **KAYAK PADDLE** has a blade on both ends. A **CANOE PADDLE** has a blade on only one end.

CANOES are **OPEN ON TOP** and can fit more **PEOPLE.**

Kayaks and canoes are fun ways to travel on the water. Paddling pushes a boat forward through the water. The paddle is also used for steering. The faster you paddle, the faster you'll go!

People ride a paddleboard standing up. This sport takes good balance.

15

WIND POWER

Specially designed **SAILS** help **RACING SAILBOATS** like these **ZIP ALONG** with the **WIND.**

Sails catch the wind to move boats forward through water. As long as the wind blows, sailboats can go. Sailors began taking long sea voyages about 5,000 years ago. The first sailboats had one sail.

CHINESE JUNK
SAILBOAT

Chinese sailboats called junks were some of the first boats with sails that went up and down. In bad weather, sailors lower the sails.

A big sailing ship needs a big push to go. A clipper ship has many sails to catch a lot of wind. Each sail is connected to a long pole called a mast. Sailors use ropes attached to the sails to raise and lower them.

How would you describe the strongest wind you have ever felt?

Lowered sails are **FURLED,** or **FOLDED,** for storage. **UNPACKING** a sail is called **UNFURLING.**

CLIPPER SHIP

17

ACROSS SNOW AND ICE

Here are some ways people go—and have fun–when snow covers the ground and lakes and rivers freeze hard.

ICEBOAT

CROSS-COUNTRY SKIS

SNOWBOARD

ON THE GO

SLED

DOGSLED

SNOWSHOES

ICE SKATES

19

LET'S PLAY A GAME!

Find all the things that go on land. How many of these things go on water? How many go on snow or ice?

CHAPTER 2
LET IT ROLL

The invention of the wheel made it a lot easier to get from place to place on land.

ROLL IT!

Why is it so hard to drag something heavy over the ground? It's because of a force called friction. Friction happens when two objects rub against each other. The more rubbing, the more friction, and the harder it is to move something.

When an object is pulled on a sledge or rolled along on logs or wheels, there's not as much rubbing against the ground. That means there's less friction, and the load can be moved faster and more easily.

WHEELS reduce **FRICTION**, so the suitcase is **EASIER** to move over the ground.

SLEDGE

LOG ROLLERS

Before there were wheels, it took a group of strong people or animals to drag heavy loads over rough ground. Putting a load on a sledge with runners or rolling it over logs made the job easier.

FRICTION makes it hard to **DRAG** a **HEAVY** load.

25

WHEELING AROUND

SPOKES make **WHEELS** lightweight and **STRONG.**

Spokes

Thousands of years ago, people started using carts and wagons with wheels. Wheels made it easier and faster to move food, building materials, and many other things from one place to another. Wheeled wagons and carts were powered by people and animals. They still are sometimes.

IT TAKES PUSHING OR PULLING TO GET WHEELS ROLLING.

JOGGING STROLLER: pushed on three wheels

RICKSHAW: pulled on two wheels

WHEELBARROW: pushed on one wheel

WAGON: pulled on four wheels

In **ANCIENT** times, **HORSES PULLED** two-wheeled carts called **CHARIOTS** in **RACES** and **BATTLES.**

The **FIRST WHEELS** were made of **HEAVY,** solid wood.

What do you push or pull that has wheels? How many wheels does it have?

27

GIDDYAP!

Before trains and cars came into use, horse-drawn carriages called stagecoaches were the speediest way to travel long distances. The coaches made quick stops at stations along the way to change horses. After tired horses had eaten and rested, they were hitched up to the next coach.

The driver's **SEAT** of a **STAGECOACH** hid a **TREASURE** box for **GOLD** and other **PRECIOUS** goods.

How does your family travel long distances?

Clang, clang! Out of the way! Firefighters raced to fires on horse-drawn wagons. A bell on the fire wagon sounded the alarm.

FIRE WAGON

PEOPLE RODE inside the **STAGECOACH** or on the **ROOF** with the **LUGGAGE.**

Fancy royal carriages have carried kings and queens for hundreds of years. The queen of Great Britain traveled to her crowning ceremony in the Gold State Coach.

Great Britain's Gold State Coach is so heavy it takes eight horses to pull it.

PEDAL POWER

The first bike, called the balance bike or dandy horse, didn't have pedals. To make the wheels go, riders pushed with their feet on the ground.

Later inventors attached pedals to bikes. The "ordinary" bicycle had a very big front wheel with pedals and a very small back wheel.

BALANCE BIKE

It was a **LONG WAY DOWN** if you **FELL** off the **ORDINARY BIKE!**

TODAY'S **BIKES** have pedals that **TURN** a **CHAIN.** The chain turns the **REAR WHEEL.**

CHAIN

IT'S A RACE!

The Tour de France is one of the world's longest bike races. It takes place over 23 days. Riders go up and down mountains and hills as they pedal through several countries in Europe. The finish line is always in Paris, France.

Which of these bikes do you think can go fastest?

On a **SURREY BIKE,** also called a **PEDAL CAR,** everybody **PEDALS.**

Bicycles aren't the only things that need pedal power to go. Here are some more examples of wheeled vehicles with pedals.

Which of these vehicles would you like to ride?

Tricycles, or trikes, have three wheels.

Pedicabs, also called bike taxis, are a popular way to see the sights in some cities.

A unicycle has only one wheel.

BMX BIKES

These sturdy bikes are used in bicycle motocross (BMX) racing. Riders compete on a special track filled with jumps, turns, and obstacles. BMX racing is an Olympic sport for men and women.

33

KEEP ON ROLLING

Unless they're going downhill, roller skates, skateboards, and scooters all need people power to make them move. To get going, riders push off from the ground with one foot, then roll.

ROLLER SKATES, also called QUAD SKATES, have two wheels in **FRONT** and two wheels in **BACK.**

INLINE SKATES have **TWO** to **FIVE WHEELS** in a **SINGLE LINE.**

Scooters are for play—and also for getting to work!

The first **SKATEBOARDS** were made by attaching **ROLLER SKATE WHEELS** to the bottom of a **WOODEN BOARD.**

ON THE COURT

Wheelchair basketball players dribble, shoot, guard, and race across courts in specially designed wheelchairs.

LET'S PLAY A GAME!

A pattern is something that repeats. The wheeled vehicles make three patterns in the three rows in this game. Can you say which vehicle belongs in each of the three empty circles?

2 HARDER

ROLLER SKATES • SKATEBOARD • WAGON • ROLLER SKATES • SKATEBOARD

3 HARDEST

BICYCLE • BMX BIKES • BICYCLE • SCOOTER • BICYCLE

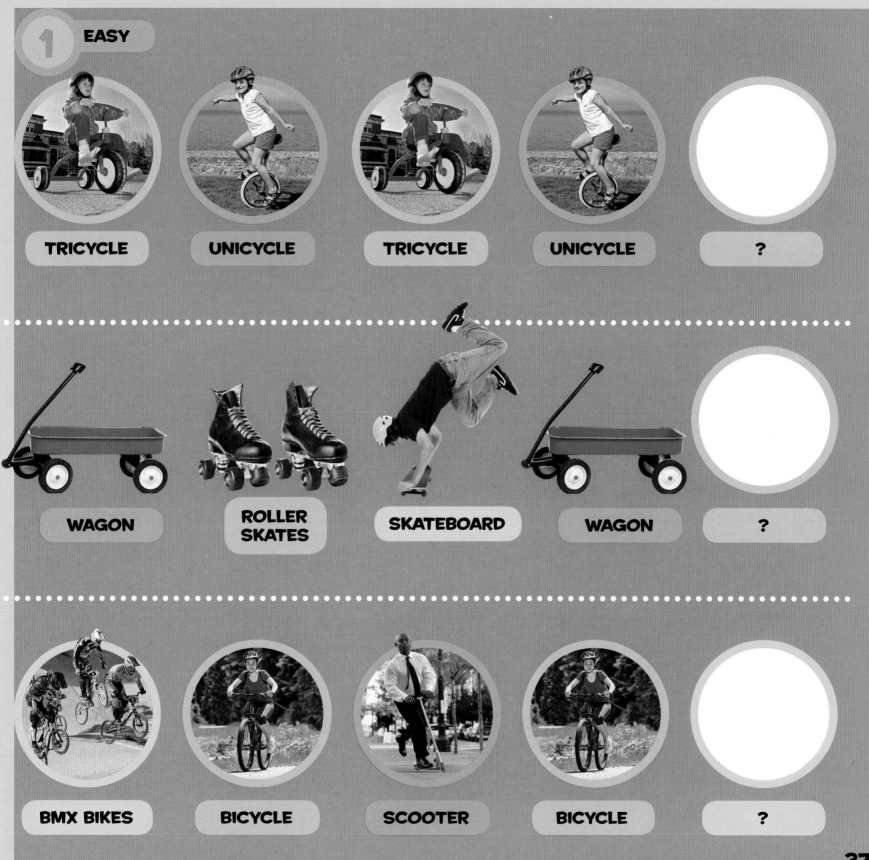

TRICYCLE UNICYCLE TRICYCLE UNICYCLE ?

WAGON ROLLER SKATES SKATEBOARD WAGON ?

BMX BIKES BICYCLE SCOOTER BICYCLE ?

CHAPTER 3
POWERING UP

Humans, horses, and other animals can use their muscles to make things go over land, but engines are more powerful.

FROM HORSES TO ENGINES

Horses can pull all kinds of vehicles, but they need a lot of care and food—not to mention having to clean up after them! Engines started replacing horses for "go" power about 200 years ago.

Engines are machines that turn energy into motion, or movement. They get their energy from burning different types of fuel. The energy is given off as heat.

KIDS need **FUEL** to **RUN** and **PLAY.**

What's your favorite fuel?
(HINT: Food is fuel for humans and animals.)

Horses fuel up on hay, grass, and oats. Apples and carrots are favorite treats.

wood

coal

Early **ENGINES** used **WOOD** or **COAL** as **FUEL.**

41

STEAM MACHINES

"Go blow off some **STEAM**" means "go let out some **ENERGY**."

The **ENGINE** that moves **RAILROAD** cars on a **TRACK** is called a locomotive.

All aboard! The first trains were called iron horses. They were powered by engines that made steam by burning coal or wood to heat water.

Can you make a steam whistle sound? Try it!

Boiling **HOT** water makes **STEAM.**

POWERING UP

engineer

fireman

It takes at least two people to run a steam engine. The fireman keeps the coal or wood burning hot. An engineer drives the train. To signal the train is coming, the engineer pulls a cord that lets steam through a whistle: *Whoo, whoo!*

IRON HORSE RACE

A small train named *Tom Thumb* raced against a horse nearly 200 years ago to prove the power of steam engines. Both the train and the horse pulled passenger cars. *Tom Thumb* went faster, but when it broke down, the horse won the race.

43

MORE STEAM MACHINES

Powerful steam traction engines, called tractors, plowed fields and hauled logs more than 100 years ago.

STEAM TRACTORS took the place of **HORSES** on some farms. Today most tractors are powered by **DIESEL FUEL.**

STEAM CAR

STEAM CAR

FULL STEAM AHEAD!

Here's how the first steam engines worked.

2. The fire heats the water to make steam.

3. The hot steam goes through pipes to push on the piston.

1. Coal or wood is burned in the firebox.

4. The piston is connected to a rod that turns the wheels.

More than half the cars in the United States used to run on steam power, too. Inventors are now working on new kinds of steam-powered cars.

45

STEAMBOATS

Steamboats chug along rivers and lakes. A steam engine turns a giant paddle wheel to push the boat. Most paddle wheels are at the back of the boat, but some are on the side.

STEAMBOAT

Steamships like the *Queen Mary* cruised across the ocean by steam power. Some of these big steamships still sail today, but newer ocean liners run on diesel-powered engines.

PEOPLE often give **NAMES** to **BOATS** and **SHIPS.**

STEAMSHIP

POWERING UP

SPINNING BY STEAM

Steam can spin a propeller to make a big ship go. Look at the huge propeller on this ship.

If you had a boat, what would you name it?

47

IT'S ELECTRIC!

This early electric car was cone-shaped at both ends.

The first **ELECTRIC VEHICLES** were called **HORSELESS CARRIAGES.**

An Electrobat may sound like a cool new toy, but it is actually an old-style electric car that sparked excitement more than 100 years ago.

In an electric car, the motor is powered by electricity stored in batteries. When the batteries run out of power, they have to be replaced or recharged.

ELECTROBAT

TESLA ELECTRIC CAR

Some **ELECTRIC CARS** today can go for **200 MILES** (322 km) or more on a single **BATTERY CHARGE.**

CITICAR ELECTRIC CAR

Early electric taxicabs were nicknamed "hummingbirds" because the motors made a sound like the whirring of a hummingbird's wings.

BATTERY POWER

Cars aren't the only things that use battery power to go. Here are some more battery-powered vehicles.

GOLF **CARTS** carry golfers and their equipment around a **GOLF COURSE.**

BATTERY-OPERATED TOY CAR

ALVIN

OCEAN SCIENTISTS dive down **DEEP** in **ALVIN.** This **BATTERY-POWERED SUBMERSIBLE** can go **10 HOURS** before it needs **RECHARGING.**

SEGWAYS

What other things can you think of that move using battery power?

An **ELECTRIC BIKE** has a small **MOTOR** that helps riders go **FARTHER** and **FASTER** with less **PEDAL POWER.**

51

RIDING
THE RAILS

CARREIRA Nº

573

565

STREETCARS

Steam trains made a lot of smoke from burning coal or wood in the firebox. They also made a lot of noise.

Today, many trains have giant electric motors, which are quieter and cleaner. The electricity that powers the motors comes from an electrical rail on the ground or from overhead electrical wires.

TROLLEY BUS

Underground subway trains in New York City use electricity from a rail on the ground.

This **COMMUTER TRAIN** gets **ELECTRICITY** from overhead **WIRES.**

MOVING ON CABLES

Some things that go get a ride on strong wire ropes called cables. Electric motors keep the cables constantly moving around in giant loops.

In San Francisco, California, U.S.A., cable cars take passengers up and down the hilly streets. A special claw under the car grips the cable moving below the street. The cable pulls the car along with it.

CABLE CAR

Would you rather walk up a very steep hill or ride up in a cable car?

FUNICULAR

A cable railcar called a funicular (foo-NICK-u-lahr) carries passengers up and down steep hills in some cities.

Chairlifts carry skiers and sightseers up and down mountain slopes.

GONDOLA

Gondolas, tramways, and chairlifts are hanging cable cars. Giant cables tow them high above the ground.

55

GOING THE DISTANCE . . . FAST!

Don't blink, or you might miss it! A superfast electric train can zoom along at 350 miles an hour (563 km/h). That's faster than some airplanes.

If you were riding in a train, would you rather be in the first car or the last car? Why?

HIGH-SPEED trains like this one are called **"BULLET TRAINS."**

These trains use special wheel systems and extra-smooth rails to move so quickly. They have pointed noses, like arrows, to help them zip down the track.

POWERING UP

MAGNETS, NOT MAGIC

How do you make a train float through the air? If you said magic, think again. It's magnets! Super speedy maglev trains use electromagnets to go.

Magnets that are different stick together. Magnets that are alike push apart, or repel each other. The magnets on the bottom of a maglev train repel electromagnets on the track. This push lifts the train off the track a little.

ZOOM! MAGLEV trains can travel at **375** miles an hour (603 km/h).

57

LET'S PLAY A GAME!

Match each type of transportation to what gives it the energy it needs to go.

WOOD AND COAL

ELECTRICITY

ELECTROMAGNETS

HAY AND GRASS

BATTERY POWER

STEAM TRAIN

MAGLEV TRAIN

TROLLEY BUS

HORSES

ALVIN SUBMERSIBLE

CHAPTER 4
FIRE IT UP!

Today, most vehicles get their power from gasoline-powered engines.

ENERGY FROM GASOLINE

About a hundred years ago, when the first electric cars were zipping around, inventors were also making vehicles powered by gasoline, a liquid fuel.

The Benz Patent Motor Car from 1886 had three wheels and ran using the first gas-powered engine.

Gasoline burns inside a car's engine, creating bursts of energy that give the car "go" power.

This Duryea automobile had four wheels and ran on gas.

One of the earliest—and most popular—gas-powered cars was the Ford Model T. It was the first car put together on a moving assembly line. Each worker along the assembly line had a job: to put one part of the car into place as it passed on a moving belt.

GASOLINE and **DIESEL** are **LIQUID FUELS** made from **OIL**. Some **CARS** and **TRUCKS** run on diesel fuel.

Ford Model T assembly line

63

CAR COLLECTION

CONVERTIBLE

MINIVAN

SEDAN

The Ford Model T and the Benz Patent Motor Car are cool cars from long ago. Today's cars are much faster, quieter, more comfortable, easier to control, and safer. Here are a few kinds of cars you might see around on roads today.

SPORT-UTILITY VEHICLE

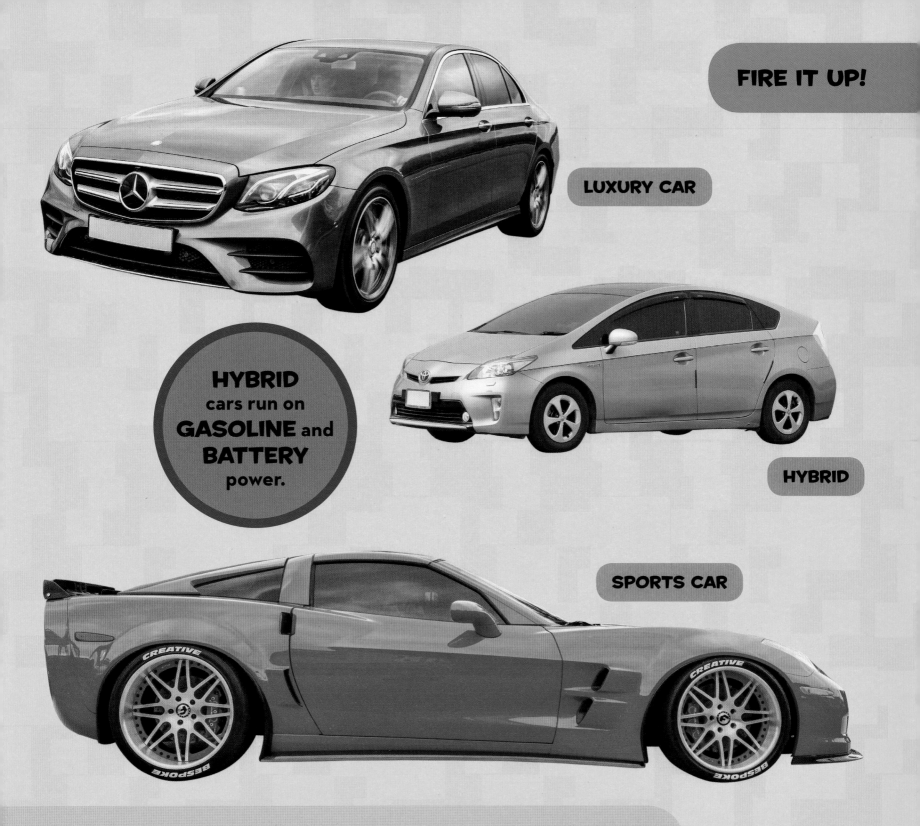

FIRE IT UP!

LUXURY CAR

HYBRID
cars run on
GASOLINE and
BATTERY
power.

HYBRID

SPORTS CAR

How many of these cars have you seen?

ON THE ROAD

You can spot many kinds of cars when you're on the road. Depending on where you live, here are a few other gas-powered vehicles you might see when you're out and about. Make a game of seeing how many different things that go you can count each time you head out. Try looking for trucks, motorcycles, emergency vehicles, and more!

AMBULANCE

AMBULANCE

AMBULANCES come **QUICKLY** if someone needs to **GET TO THE HOSPITAL** right away.

ICE-CREAM TRUCK

CONES · SHAKES · SUNDAES

FUN-TIME

TOW TRUCK

FIRE IT UP!

A street **SWEEPER** has big **BROOMS** that spin along the side of a **ROAD** to sweep up **GARBAGE** and dirt.

GARBAGE TRUCK

Amphibious vehicles can drive on land like a bus or car, and go into water to float like a boat.

Police officers **ZOOM** to emergencies in special **POLICE CARS** with **SIRENS** and flashing **LIGHTS.**

Motorcycles like this one are **DESIGNED** for **RIDING ON STREETS.**

Delivery trucks carry packages and letters from one place to another.

Construction sites need **DUMP TRUCKS** to transport **ROCKS** and **DIRT.**

69

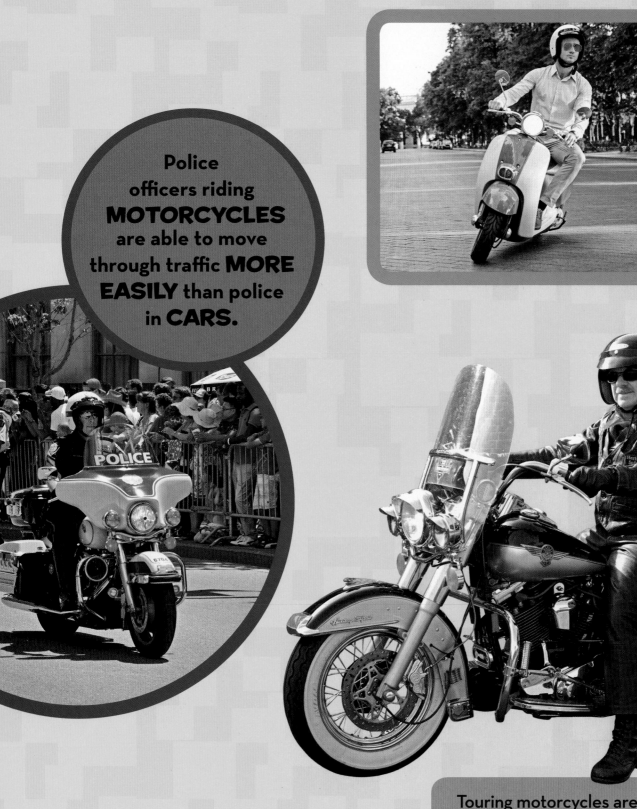

Scooters are smaller than motorcycles. They are also a lot quieter!

Police officers riding **MOTORCYCLES** are able to move through traffic **MORE EASILY** than police in **CARS.**

Touring motorcycles are designed for long-distance travel. They have screens to block wind, big tanks for fuel, and room for luggage.

SCHOOL BUS

STOP

3

Some **KIDS** ride a **SCHOOL BUS** to and from **SCHOOL.**

Recreational vehicles, known as RVs, allow people to drive and live in a vehicle they can take on vacation. RVs have kitchens, bathrooms, living spaces, and bedrooms. This is a small one, but RVs come in many sizes.

PICKUP TRUCKS are used to haul construction **MATERIALS,** hardware, machinery, **FURNITURE,** trees and **PLANTS,** and much more.

71

A taxicab driver is paid to take passengers where they need to go.

TANKER TRUCKS deliver GASOLINE to gas stations.

When **HORSES** need to be **MOVED** from **ONE PLACE** to **ANOTHER**, their owners use a **HORSE VAN** to get them there.

A concrete-mixer truck's spinning drum mixes cement, sand, and water as it drives to a construction site.

DRUM

DIRT BIKES are built to drive **OFF-ROAD** in dirt, sand, mud, and snow.

Which of the vehicles you've just read about would you like to ride in or on?

73

IT'S A RACE!

CARS like these compete in the **INDY 500**, a race held every year on a track in **INDIANAPOLIS**, Indiana, U.S.A.

Ready, steady, go! Car racing has been around as long as there have been cars to drive. Race cars today compete on special tracks, where people can watch safely.

The Monaco Grand Prix tests Formula 1 cars on a twisty course just over two miles (3.2 km) long. Low, fast Formula 1 cars zoom up and down hills and through tunnels, over and over 78 times.

The **MONACO GRAND PRIX** race is held every year in **MONACO**, a city-state in **EUROPE.**

NASCAR stands for National Association for Stock Car Auto Racing. Stock cars may look like regular cars, but they are made in special factories that build them with parts made just for racing. They have powerful engines and lots of safety features.

Cars whiz around the track at a NASCAR race in Talladega, Alabama, U.S.A.

REARVIEW MIRRORS were originally made for race cars. Now **EVERY CAR** has one for safety.

The first car race in the United States took place in Illinois in 1895. Six cars raced 54 miles (87 km). It took the winner almost eight hours to finish. Nowadays, a race of that distance would take way less than one hour to complete.

Close your eyes and imagine driving a race car. Would you rather race on an oval track or on a twisty, hilly track?

77

LET'S PLAY A GAME!

Use the pictures to help you read this story about vehicles on the road.

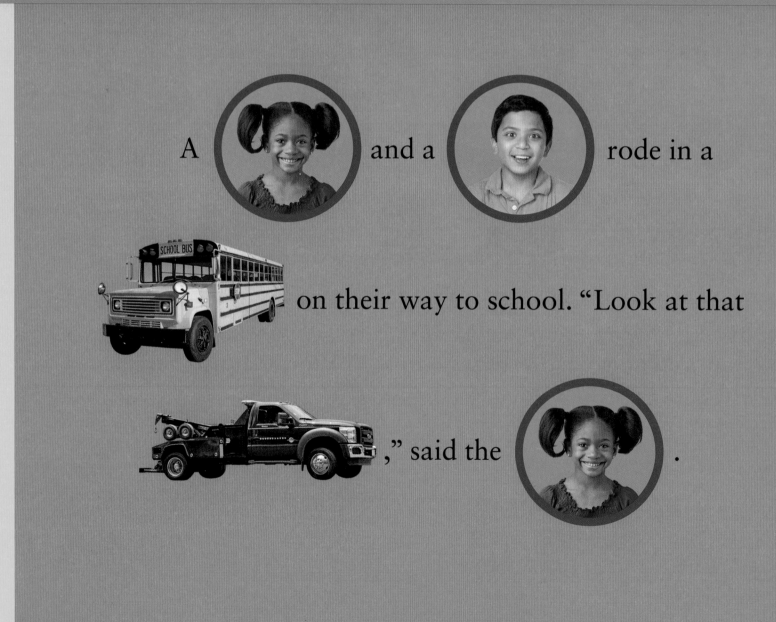

A 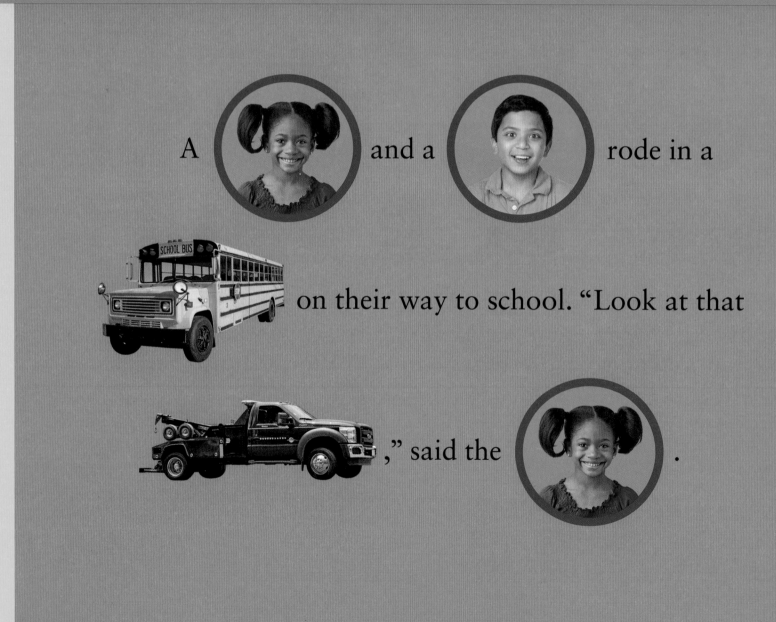 and a rode in a

 on their way to school. "Look at that

," said the .

"That 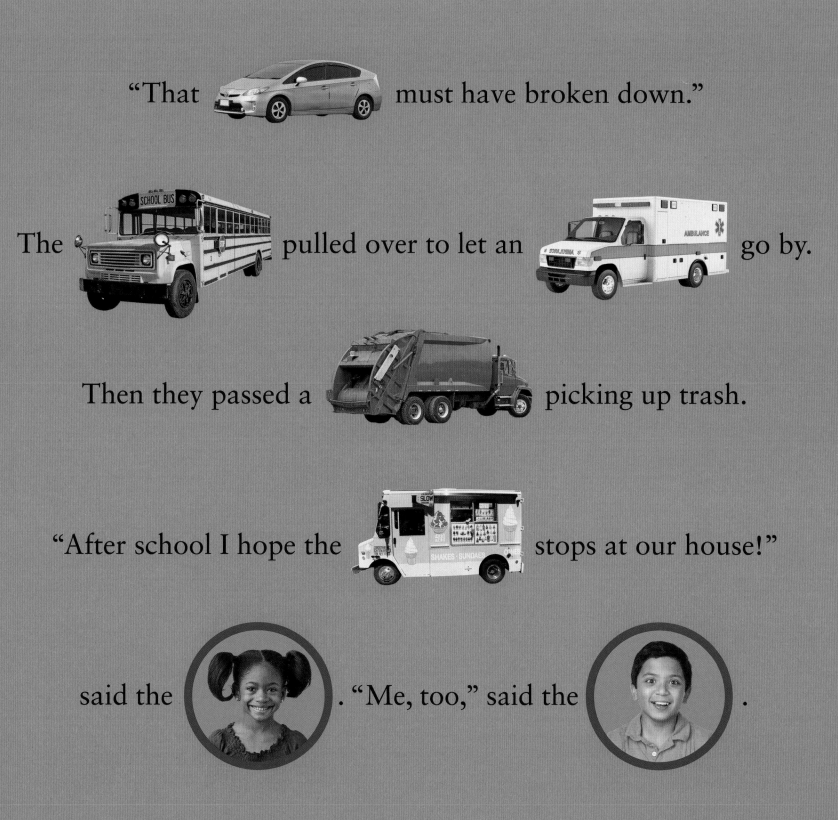 must have broken down."

The pulled over to let an go by.

Then they passed a picking up trash.

"After school I hope the stops at our house!"

said the . "Me, too," said the .

CHAPTER 5
BIG AND BIGGER

On land or in the sea, built for work or built for fun,
the biggest things that go are awesome!

ON THE LAND

Tractor-trailers move all kinds of heavy loads, including huge shipping containers filled with everything from toys to sneakers to furniture to bananas.

Lots of people travel to and from work and school on city buses. Sometimes these buses are extra long, with a folded accordion middle to help them go around tight corners.

TRACTOR-TRAILERS

ACCORDION BUS

ACCORDION

Fire! *Honk, Honk!* Fire engines carry firefighters and gear to a fire. A ladder truck is extra long. It lifts a motorized ladder to a window or roof high on a building.

TRACTOR-TRAILERS are also called **BIG RIGS** and **18-WHEELERS.**

LADDER TRUCK

Which of these vehicles have you seen on roads near you?

IN THE WATER

CONTAINER
SHIP

A cruise ship is like a floating city for thousands of people. It has stores, theaters, swimming pools, restaurants, and hotel-style rooms for people to sleep in.

Huge container ships carry shipping containers across the seas from one country to another. When a ship gets into port, the containers are transferred to freight trains or tractor-trailers.

Oil tankers are some of the longest ships in the world.

How many of these ships are built for work?

An **AIRCRAFT CARRIER** has a large deck where **PLANES** can take off and land.

85

SNOWCAT

RAKE

4.5

600

TREADS

ON ICE AND SNOW

A snowcat grips the snow with big treads to climb steep ski slopes. It drags a big snow rake to groom the trails.

Giant tundra vehicles are specially designed to travel over frozen ground. From them, visitors can see polar bears safely.

An **ICE RESURFACER** is used to **SMOOTH** out the ice on a **SKATING RINK.**

An **ICEBREAKER** is a ship that clears an opening through **THICK ICE** in frozen waters.

TUNDRA VEHICLE

ON THE FARM

PLOW

TRACTOR

A tractor pushes, pulls, tows, and more. Farmers use tractors to help them plant and harvest food. This tractor is pulling a plow. The plow prepares the soil for planting.

What foods do you eat that come from farms?

Farmers use machines called **COMBINES** to **HARVEST CROPS** such as wheat and corn.

A **COTTON HARVESTER** picks cotton and packs it in **NEAT ROUND BALES.**

89

AT THE CONSTRUCTION SITE

Some of the most gigantic things that go are found at construction sites.

Front-end loaders scoop up loads using a huge front bucket. The biggest ones are two stories tall and can lift enough rocks and dirt to fill five ordinary-size dump trucks in one load.

FRONT-END LOADER

CRAWLER DOZERS have a BIG FRONT BLADE to MOVE DIRT and other materials.

Giant DUMP TRUCKS like this one haul huge loads of ROCKS AND COAL dug from mines.

COMPACTORS FLATTEN the surface of roads as they are being built. The HEAVY ROLLERS make a smooth surface.

91

HOMES ON THE GO

A motor home is a large RV. Families can go on vacation with everything they need in their motor home. They can even tow a car to use to explore their favorite spot.

Travel trailers are another kind of home you can take on the road to live in. These trailers attach to a car or truck that pulls them along.

TRAVEL TRAILER

LET'S PLAY A GAME!

With your finger, follow the path that takes each vehicle where it needs to go.

CHAPTER 6
IN THE AIR

There are many ways to go in the air. Let's fly!

UP, UP, AND AWAY!

For thousands of years, people could only dream of flying. Then about 240 years ago, inventors figured out how to go up—in a balloon!

The first balloon flight with human passengers lifted off in France in 1783. It flew for 25 minutes and went 5.5 miles (9 km). The huge balloon was filled with hot air from a fire to make it rise. As the air cooled, the balloon sank back to Earth.

Before the first **HOT-AIR BALLOON** went up with **PEOPLE** on board, a test flight safely carried a **DUCK**, a **ROOSTER**, and a **SHEEP**.

Hot air is **LIGHTER** than cold air. So when the air outside a balloon is **COLDER** than the air inside it, the balloon **FLOATS.**

In hot-air balloons today, a burner heats the air during a flight, so the balloon can stay up longer. A fireproof skirt protects the balloon from catching fire.

BURNER

FIREPROOF SKIRT

BASKET FOR CARRYING FUEL, PILOT, AND PASSENGERS

Can you name more than three colors in the balloons in this picture?

99

PROPELLER

GONDOLA

PROPELLERS on the side and rear of an **AIRSHIP** move it forward and backward. Airships are also called **ZEPPELINS.**

AIRSHIPS

Giant **PARADE** balloons are also filled with **HELIUM GAS.**

Airships rise into the air like balloons, but instead of hot air, they are filled with a gas called helium, which is lighter than air. Unlike a balloon, an airship has a lightweight frame, or skeleton, on the inside. The pilot and passengers ride in a car, called a gondola, attached to the underside of the aircraft.

100

GLIDERS

SAILPLANE

A sailplane **PILOT** rides inside the **AIRCRAFT.**

Gliders don't have engines, so they need help getting up into the air. Once they are up there, they ride the wind with their wings. A sailplane is a glider that gets towed high into the sky by an airplane with an engine. Once the sailplane is high enough, it is unhooked and flies on its own.

A hang-glider pilot runs and jumps off a tall cliff to catch the wind. Eventually the glider drifts down, and the pilot steers it to land on the ground.

HANG GLIDER

A **HANG-GLIDER** pilot hangs below the wings in a special **HARNESS** and steers with the triangle-shaped **CONTROL BAR.**

101

FLYING MACHINES

Orville Wright piloted **FLYER** on its first **SUCCESSFUL FLIGHT.** He lay flat on his belly on top of the lower wing to work the controls.

Brothers Orville and Wilbur Wright were the first inventors to figure out how to make an airplane lift off from the ground on its own power and fly. It was on a windy day in 1903 at the beach in Kitty Hawk, North Carolina, U.S.A. Powered by a lightweight engine, their plane—called *Flyer*—flew about the length of two and a half American football fields in one minute.

102

Try, try again. That's how people invent things. There were a lot of creative airplane designs in the early days. Some worked. Some did not.

MULTIPLANE

MULTIPLANE

COLLAPSIBLE GLIDER

If you could fly an airplane, where is the first place you would go?

103

PROPELLER POWER

It only takes one set of wings to get off the ground, but some planes have more. There are many different kinds of airplanes flying around today. Here are just a few that use propellers for power.

Loop-de-loop! **STUNT PLANES** do **SPINS** and **FLY LOOPS** in the sky.

PROPELLER

A **BIPLANE** has two sets of wings. The wing **ON TOP** is a **SINGLE** wing that goes **ALL THE WAY** across.

TRIPLANES have **THREE** wings and can **SWOOP** and **ZIP** around in the sky.

PONTOON

Seaplanes use propellers to get up enough speed to take off from the surface of the water. Instead of wheels, they have pontoons for takeoff and landing.

JET POWER

Faster and faster! Airplanes take millions of people to different places every day. Propeller planes are still around, but these days most airplanes use jet engines. Powerful jet engines allow planes to fly faster and higher than propeller planes.

The **HEINKEL HE 178** was the **FIRST JET-POWERED** plane. Its first flight was in **1939.**

The Airbus A380 plane is the biggest passenger jet in the air today. It can carry more than 850 passengers.

The first 747 jumbo jet flew about 50 years ago. This kind of plane is taller than a six-story building and can hold up to 550 passengers.

Can you count how many airplanes you see in one day?

The U.S. Navy's **BLUE ANGELS** aerobatic team of pilots fly powerful jets called **HORNETS.** The pilots fly in **TRICKY FORMATIONS** at air shows.

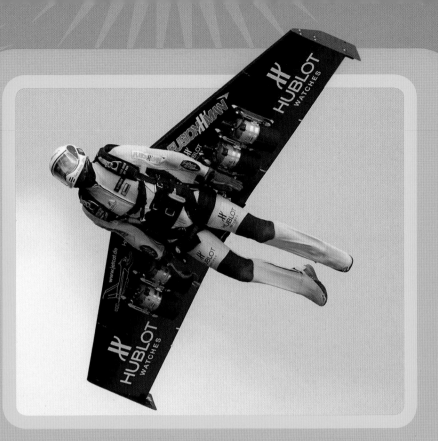

He's not a superhero, but this is super cool! Yves Rossy, also called the Jetman, is a pilot who invented a jet pack. With his jet-powered wings strapped to his back, Rossy can spin and roll just like a stunt plane.

CONTRAIL

Harrier jets can fly straight up, hover in midair, and dash forward.

The **LONG WHITE TRAILS** left behind by jets are called **CONTRAILS.** They are made of tiny drops of **WATER** that float together in line-shaped **CLOUDS.**

HANG TIME

Thwap, thwap, thwap, thwap! It's the beating sound of a helicopter. Fast-spinning propellers lift a helicopter straight up off the ground. Helicopters can move in a lot of ways that most airplanes cannot.

Helicopters go forward and backward. They go straight up and down. They can hover, or stay put in the air, in one spot. They can even spin around and go the other way.

The **WORLD'S FASTEST** helicopter is a cross between a **PROPELLER AIRPLANE** and a **HELICOPTER.**

The **PRESIDENT** of the **UNITED STATES** travels in a helicopter called **MARINE ONE.**

UNITED STATES OF AMERICA

111

A Chinook helicopter has two propellers for double the lifting power. This Chinook is delivering big bags of sand.

Helicopters are also called **CHOPPERS** and **HELOS.**

The V22 Osprey aircraft flies like a helicopter. But it can rotate its propellers to the front to fly like a plane.

Small remote-controlled aircraft are sometimes called drones. They have lots of propellers that run on batteries.

Would you rather ride in a helicopter or an airplane? Why?

BLAST OFF!

Rockets carry spaceships, space shuttles, satellites, telescopes, and astronauts deep into space. Anything going into space needs a rocket engine's big push to get there.

A **ROCKET LIFTOFF** is also called a **LAUNCH** or **BLASTOFF.**

EXTERNAL FUEL TANK

SPACE SHUTTLE ORBITER

ROCKET BOOSTERS give extra push during **BLASTOFF.**

SOLID ROCKET BOOSTERS

When the **SPACE SHUTTLE** got far enough away from **EARTH**, the **ROCKET BOOSTERS** and **FUEL TANK** dropped away from it. The shuttle **ORBITER** continued into space.

The space shuttle launched into orbit with rocket boosters, but it landed back on Earth like a glider. For 30 years, it carried astronauts, satellites, and supplies into space. Now space shuttles are in museums.

This picture shows **SOME** of the kinds of **SATELLITES** orbiting **EARTH.**

AROUND AND AROUND

There are thousands of machines called satellites orbiting, or flying around, Earth. Some satellites take pictures of our planet. Some send phone calls and TV signals around the world.

The **HUBBLE SPACE TELESCOPE** is a school bus–size telescope orbiting Earth. It takes pictures of **FARAWAY STARS** and **GALAXIES** and sends them to scientists on **EARTH.**

The International Space Station orbits Earth once every 90 minutes. Astronauts live there for months at a time doing research. Cargo ships like the Space X Dragon deliver supplies to the astronauts.

SPACE X DRAGON

INTERNATIONAL SPACE STATION

TO THE MOON

Apollo spacecraft traveled to the moon. They had several parts. The astronauts rode in the command module on the way to the moon. While the command module orbited the moon, two of the astronauts unhooked the lunar module. They traveled in the lunar module to the moon's surface and then flew it back to the command module, which took them all back to Earth.

COMMAND MODULE

LUNAR MODULE

Astronauts explored the moon **BY FOOT** and in a **WHEELED VEHICLE** called the lunar rover.

LUNAR means "of the moon."

LUNAR ROVER

SIX Apollo flights landed on the moon. The **FIRST ONE** was in **1969**. The **LAST ONE** was in **1972**.

A **SMALL ENGINE** on the Apollo lunar module **LAUNCHED** it off the moon's **SURFACE** and back to the **COMMAND** module.

What do you think it would feel like to walk on the moon?

This
Mars **ROVER,**
called **CURIOSITY,**
stretched out its
**MECHANICAL
ARM** to take a
PICTURE of
itself.

MISSION TO MARS

The United States' space agency, NASA, has sent spacecraft and rovers to check out the planet Mars. The spacecraft orbit the planet and collect information about its climate. They also take pictures to send back to scientists on Earth. The rovers are wheeled robots that work on the surface of Mars. They study its soil and rocks, and they take pictures, too. NASA's goal is to send people to Mars in the future.

NASA scientists are working on a spacecraft called Orion that will take people farther away from Earth than they have ever gone before.

What's Next?

Inventors are always thinking up new ways to explore our planet, as well as distant planets and beyond. Who knows what things *you* might invent or discover in the future!

This **PICTURE** shows what it might be like for **HUMANS** to explore the **SURFACE** of **MARS** one day.

Would you like to travel into space someday? Why or why not?

121

LET'S PLAY A GAME!

How many of these flying machines have propellers?
Find all the things that fly with wings. Which of these
things can fly into space?

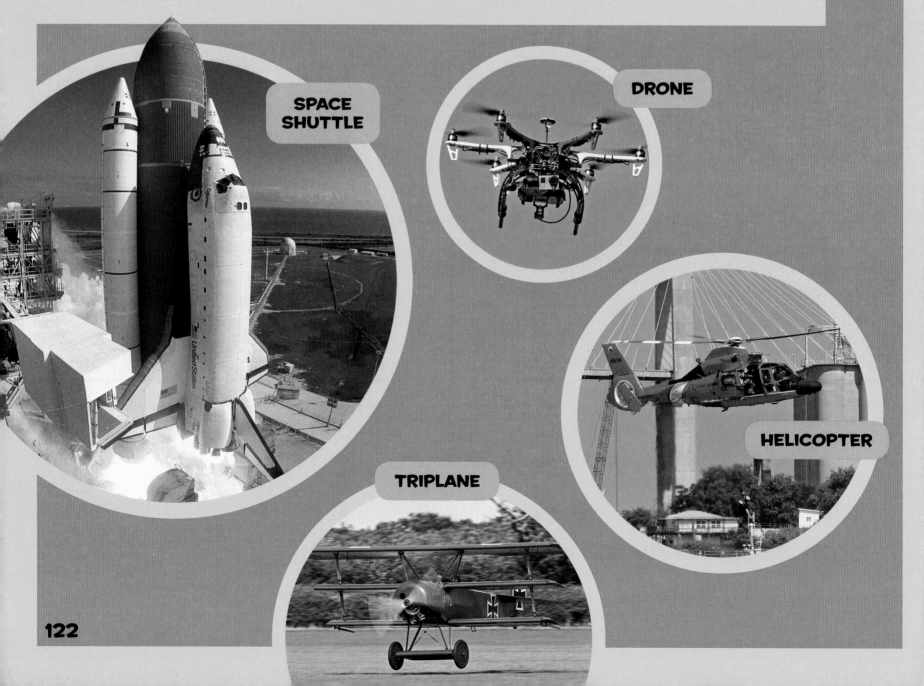

SPACE SHUTTLE

DRONE

HELICOPTER

TRIPLANE

HOT-AIR BALLOON

JETS

HANG GLIDER

LUNAR
MODULE

PARENT TIPS

Extend your child's experience beyond the pages of this book. Get outside and go. Walk to the park. Ride bikes or row a boat. Count airplanes. Invent new things. Together, you and your child can have fun and stay safe around things that go. Here are some activities you can do with National Geographic's *Little Kids First Big Book of Things That Go.*

VISIT A MUSEUM (INVESTIGATING)

There are many museums and historical sites that feature things that go. You and your child can investigate destinations online and then visit them in person. There may also be historical markers near bridges and roadways that describe who engineered a structure that helped create today's transportation system.

DESIGN A MACHINE THAT GOES (IMAGINATION AND CRAFTS)

Throughout this book are examples of inventions that helped advance—and are continuing to advance—the way we get around. Using simple materials, such as sticks, tape, and cardboard, your child can make his own creation and see if it goes. It can roll, fly, or float. Maybe it uses a pulley. The possibilities are endless.

GET OUT AND GO (MOTOR SKILLS AND EXERCISE)

Take a walk. Ride your bikes. Paddle a canoe. There are so many ways that you and your child can go for fun. Talk about how different vehicles or boats move around. Are they people-powered? Are they engine-powered? Try something new.

KEEP A FIELD JOURNAL (OBSERVING AND CATEGORIZING)

How many different vehicles do you and your child see every day? Keep a journal of what you spot on land, in the sky, and in the water. Encourage your child to draw a picture of each vehicle. Or she can cut out pictures from a magazine. See how many different parts she can label.

I SPY THINGS THAT GO (ALPHABET)

Play a game of I Spy going through the alphabet with your child. Find a vehicle for each letter as you drive on the highway or wait at the bus stop. Take turns guessing the answer.

SING GO SONGS (MUSIC)

Introduce your child to songs about things that go. Try to find a song from today and something from different eras. "Rocket Man" and "The Wheels on the Bus" are classics. The songs can be about trains, boats, airplanes, rockets, cars, roller coasters—whatever goes. You can even make up your own songs together.

GLOSSARY

ASSEMBLY LINE: a way to build objects by adding pieces in the same order each time

DIESEL: a liquid fuel made from oil

ELECTRICITY: a type of energy that happens when positive and negative charges react to each other

ELECTROMAGNET: a piece of iron wrapped in a wire coil with electricity running through it

ENERGY: the ability to move and do other types of work

ENGINE: a machine that turns heat energy into movement; similar to motor

FRICTION: a force that slows movement; caused by two objects rubbing together

FUEL: a material that releases energy

HELIUM: the gas used in some balloons and airships to make them rise

LUNAR: something that relates to the moon

MOTOR: a machine that turns heat energy into movement; similar to engine

POWER: the amount of movement or other type of work that can be done in a certain amount of time

SATELLITE: an object that moves around another object

SLEDGE: a vehicle with runners that can be pulled or pushed; similar to a sled

VEHICLE: a thing that goes; can be on the ground, in the air, in water, or in space

INDEX

CREDITS

AL = Alamy Stock Photo, DS = Dreamstime, GI = Getty Images, IS = iStockphoto, NGC = National Geographic Creative, NGS = National Geographic Staff, SS = Shutterstock

Cover (train), Tatiana Makotra/SS; (rocket), NASA; (race car), Jacom Stephens/E+/GI; (construction digger), Dmitry Kalinovsky/SS; (dog sled), Kirkgeisler/DS; (fire truck), Le Do/SS; (ship), James Steidl/SS; back cover, muratart/SS; spine, Yauhen_D/SS; 1, Anatoliy Lukich/SS; 2-3, Dmytro Aksonov/E+/GI; 4, Ammit Jack/SS; 5 (UP), topseller/SS; 5 (LO LE), Chuck Haney/DanitaDelimont.com; 5 (LO RT), dragunov/SS; 8-9, Sergey Novikov/SS; 10, NadyaEugene/SS; 11 (UP), Cathy Yeulet/IS/GI; 11 (LE), Peter Adams/Photolibrary RM/GI; 11 (LO RT), Zave Smith/Image Source/SuperStock; 12, Bartosz Hadyniak/IS/GI; 13 (UP), Damian322/DS; 13 (CTR), Paul Sutcliffe/AL; 13 (LO), De Agostini/G. Dagli Orti/GI; 14, JMichl/IS; 15 (UP), CEFutcher/IS/GI; 15 (LO), holbox/SS; 16, Shannon Hibberd/NGC; 17 (UP), cozyta/SS; 17 (LO), Regien Paassen/SS; 18 (UP), EricFerguson/IS/GI; 18 (RT), Dennis van de Water/SS; 18 (LO LE), lightpoet/SS; 19 (UP LE), ziggy_mars/IS/GI; 19 (UP RT), Alexander Piragis/DS; 19 (LO LE), Maksym Gorpenyuk/SS; 19 (LO), LWA/Dann Tardif/GI; 20 (UP LE), ziggy_mars/IS/GI; 20 (RT), Zave Smith/Image Source/SuperStock; 20 (LO LE), Shannon Hibberd/NGC; 21 (UP RT), Dennis van de Water/SS; 21 (CTR), NadyaEugene/SS; 21 (LO LE), JMichl/IS; 21 (LO RT), Regien Paassen/SS; 22-23, Jacek Chabraszewski/DS; 24, Peter Lourenco/Moment Open/GI; 25 (UP LE), H.M. Herget/NGC; 25 (UP RT), Dorling Kindersley RF/GI; 25 (LO), Graffizone/E+/GI; 26, studioworxx/IS; 27 (UP LE), nikkytok/SS; 27 (UP RT), Eddie Phantana/SS; 27 (UP RT), Celia Peterson/arabianEye/GI; 27 (LO RT), Paul Orr/SS; 27 (LO RT), Photodisc; 28, Glasshouse Images/AL; 29 (UP), Christie's Images Ltd./SuperStock; 29 (LO), Tim Graham Picture Library/GI; 30 (UP), Leemage/Corbis/GI; 30 (CTR), Library of Congress Prints and Photographs Division; 30 (LO), Monkey Business Images/SS; 31, Frederic Legrand-Comeo/SS; 32, Brocreative/SS; 33 (UP LE), John Alabaszowski/Moment Open/GI; 33 (UP CTR), Goddard New Era/AL; 33 (UP CTR), csfotoimages/IS Editorial/GI; 33 (LO), MarcelClemens/SS; 34 (LE), StockPhotosArt-Sports/AL; 34 (RT), hopsalka/IS/GI; 35 (UP LE), David Burch/Uppercut RF/GI; 35 (UP RT), Gallo Images/GI; 35 (LO), Jaimie Duplass/SS; 36-37 (skate boarder), Jaimie Duplass/SS; 36-37 (red wagon), Paul Orr/SS; 36-37 (girl on bike), Jacek Chabraszewski/DS; 36-37 (BMX bikers), MarcelClemens/SS; 36-37 (man on scooter), David Burch/Uppercut RF/GI; 37 (kid on tricycle), John Alabaszowski/GI; 38-39, ThegoodlyRooM RF/GI; 40 (FAR LEFT), Nattika/SS; 40 (FAR RIGHT), AE Pictures Inc./Stone Sub/GI; 40 (RT), Zave Smith/Image Source/SuperStock; 40 (CTR LE), oriori/SS; 40 (CTR RT), Dionisvera/SS; 41 (LO LE), spxChrome/IS; 41 (LO CTR), Alexander Levchenko/DS; 41 (LO RT), Polryaz/SS; 42, Travel Pictures Ltd/SuperStock; 43 (UP LE), Andrei Kuzmik/SS; 43 (LO), Bettmann/GI; 44, Roger Bamber/AL; 45 (UP LE), Martyn Goddard/AL; 45 (UP RT), ISC Images & Archives/GI; 46, Stephen Saks/Lonely Planet Images/GI; 46-47, Rolls Press/Popperfoto/GI; 47, Fox Photos/Hulton Archive Creative/GI; 48 (UP), Universal Images Group Editorial/UIG/GI; 48 (LO), Universal History Archive/UIG/GI; 49 (UP), dpa picture alliance/AL; 49 (LO LE), Bettmann Archive/GI; 49 (LO RT), Kts/DS; 50 (UP), Lucky Business/SS; 50 (LO RT), OlRaygun/IS/GI; 51 (UP), Kzenon/SS; 51 (LO), Niedring/Drentwett/MITO images/GI; 52 (LO LE), Emory Kristof/NGC; 52, Kiev.Victor/SS; 53 (UP LE), Justin Kase z13z/AL; 53 (UP RT), Osmany Torres Martín/SS; 53 (LO), Taina Sohlman/SS; 54, S.Borisov/SS; 55 (UP LE), mRGB/SS; 55 (UP RT), Sergey Novikov/SS; 56-57, Tang Yan Song/SS; 56-57, G. Bowater/Corbis Documentary/GI; 57, Martin Bond/Science Source; 58 (LO LE), Travel Pictures Ltd/SuperStock; 59 (UP RT), Justin Kase z13z/AL; 59 (CTR), Martin Bond/Science Source; 59 (RT), Emory Kristof/NGC; 59 (LO LE), Polryaz/SS; 60-61, Jon Feingersh/Iconica/GI; 62 (UP), Bettmann Archive/GI; 62 (LO), World History Archive/AL; 63 (UP), Harris & Ewing Collection/Library of Congress Prints and Photographs Division; 63 (LO), PhotoQuest/Archive Photos/GI; 64 (UP LE), Ovuong/SS; 64 (UP RT), Ovuong/SS; 64 (LO LE), Menno Schaefer/SS; 65 (UP), nitinut380/SS; 65 (LO), Steve Lagreca/SS; 66, DK Arts/SS; 67 (UP), anaglic/SS; 67 (CTR), nitinut380/SS; 67 (RT), Roman Tiraspolsky/SS; 67 (RT), Valentin Valkov/SS; 68 (UP), Justin Kase z11z/AL; 68 (LO), travis manley/SS; 69 (UP LE), Buzz Pictures/AL; 69 (UP RT), Supertrooper/SS; 69 (LO), Faraways/SS; 70 (UP), ESB Professional/SS; 70 (LE), jiawangkun/SS; 70 (LE), Paul Doyle/AL; 71 (UP), Stockagogo, Craig Barhorst/SS; 71 (LO LE), risteski goce/SS; 71 (LO RT), Jim Parkin/SS; 72 (UP), agap/SS; 72 (LO), Pixelci/SS; 73 (UP), Blanscape/SS; 73 (CTR), Lucian Milasan/AL; 73 (LO), Nachaliti/SS; 74, HodagMedia/SS; 75, Lars Baron/GI; 76, Jeff Greenberg/UIG/GI; 77, National Museum of American History & Smithsonian Institution Archives; 78 (UP LE), Rebecca Hale, NGS; 78 (UP RT), Rebecca Hale, NGS; 78 (CTR), Karen Katrjyan/SS; 79 (UP LE), B Christopher/AL; 79 (UP RT), Karen Katrjyan/SS; 79 (CTR), kozmoat98/IS/GI; 79 (LO CTR), Federico Rostagno/SS; 79 (LO LE), Rebecca Hale, NGS; 79 (LO RT), Rebecca Hale, NGS; 79, nitinut380/SS; 80-81, ewg3D/IS/GI; 82, Art Konovalov/SS; 82-83 (UP), Mike Flippo/SS; 82-83 (LO), joloei/SS; 83, Pierre Rochon photography/AL; 84 (UP), NAN728/SS; 84 (LO), dan_prat/Vetta/GI; 85 (UP), Gerard Koudenburg/AL; 85 (LO), Mass Communication Specialist Seaman Apprentice Krystofer Belknap/U.S. Navy; 86, Jaroslav Moravcik/SS; 87, imageBROKER/AL; 87 (LO), Richard Levine/AL; 87 (LO LE), Public Affairs Specialist 2nd Class NyxoLyno Cangemi/U.S. Coast Guard; 88, oticki/SS; 89 (UP), smereka/SS; 89 (LO), Jonas Boethling/AL; 90, Blackfox Images/AL; 91 (UP), Alexander Davidyuk/SS; 91 (CTR), Stockr/SS; 91 (LO), LeitWolf/SS; 92 (UP), Philip Lange/SS; 92 (LO), JaySi/SS; 93, Richard Broadwell/SS; 94 (UP LE), TFoxFoto/SS; 94 (UP RT), Art Konovalov/SS; 94 (LO LE), imagebroker/AL; 95 (UP), Pär Edlund/DS; 95 (CTR LE), Blue Images/Corbis RM Stills/GI; 95 (CTR RT), A_Lesik/SS; 95 (LO), Girodjl/SS; 96-97, Johnny Adolphson/SS; 98, Mary Evans Picture Library/AL; 99 (UP), topseller/SS; 99 (LO), Nicolas Raymond/SS; 100 (UP), Thierry Grun-Aero/AL; 100 (LO), lev radin/SS; 101 (UP), David Wall Photo/Lonely Planet Images/GI; 101 (LO), Tony Garcia/Image Source/GI; 102, Library of Congress Prints and Photographs Division; 103 (UP LE), Hulton Collection/GI; 103 (UP RT), Hulton Archive/GI; 104 (UP), David Acosta Allely/SS; 104 (LO), Kletr/SS; 104 (LO), Mansell Collection/TimePix/Time & Life Pictures/GI; 105 (UP), IanC66/SS; 105 (LO), ERainbow/SS; 106, best images/SS; 107 (UP), Interfoto/AL; 107 (CTR), Cylonphoto/IS Editorial/GI; 107 (LO), muratart/SS; 108, Petty Officer 1st Class Daniel M. Young/U.S. Navy; 109 (UP LE), Fabrice Coffrini/AFP/GI; 109 (LO LE), Photographer's Mate 3rd Class Stephanie M. Bergman/U.S. Navy; 109 (RT), Petty Officer 1st Class Daniel M. Young/U.S. Navy; 110, Petty Officer 3rd Class Ross Ruddell/U.S. Coast Guard; 111 (UP), Wolfgang Kumm/AFP/GI; 111 (LO), PHC C.M. Fitzpatrick/U.S. Marine Corps; 112 (UP), Sgt. Brian Cooper, 2nd Battalion, 135th Aviation Regiment, Colorado Army National Guard/U.S. Army; 112 (LO), Senior Airman Julianne Showalter/U.S. Air Force; 113, Alexey Yuzhakov/SS; 114, NASA; 115, 3DSculptor/IS/GI; 116, NASA; 117 (UP), NASA; 117 (LO LE), NASA; 117 (LO RT), Tim Peake/ESA/NASA/GI; 118 (UP), John Ortmann/NASA; 118 (LO), Harrison H. Schmitt/NASA; 119, David R. Scott/NASA; 120 (UP), JPL-Caltech/MSSNASA; 120 (LO), NASA; 121 (LE), Stuart O'Sullivan/The Image Bank/GI; 121 (RT), Peter Bollinger; 122 (UP LE), Kennedy Space Center/NASA; 122 (UP RT), Photodynamx/DS; 122 (CTR RT), U.S. Coast Guard, Official Photograph; 122 (LO), IanC66/SS; 123 (UP LE), Johan Knelsen/SS; 123 (UP RT), Petty Officer 1st Class Daniel M. Young/U.S. Navy; 123 (LO LE), Johnson Space Center/NASA; 123 (LO RT), vuk8691/GI; 128, Jacek Chabraszewski/SS

For all young inventors who are imagining new ways of moving technology forward, faster and farther than we can envision today. —KdS

Since 1888, the National Geographic Society has funded more than 12,000 research, exploration, and preservation projects around the world. The Society receives funds from National Geographic Partners, LLC, funded in part by your purchase. A portion of the proceeds from this book supports this vital work. To learn more, visit natgeo.com/info.

For more information, visit nationalgeographic.com, call 1-800-647-5463, or write to the following address:

National Geographic Partners 1145 17th Street N.W. Washington, D.C. 20036-4688 U.S.A.

Visit us online at nationalgeographic.com/books

For librarians and teachers: ngchildrensbooks.org

More for kids from National Geographic: kids.nationalgeographic.com

For information about special discounts for bulk purchases, please contact National Geographic Books Special Sales: specialsales@natgeo.com

For rights or permissions inquiries, please contact National Geographic Books Subsidiary Rights: bookrights@natgeo.com

Art directed by Brett Challos
Designed by Yay! Design

Hardcover ISBN: 978-1-4263-2804-6

Reinforced library edition ISBN: 978-1-4263-2805-3

Printed in China 17/PPS/1

The author would like to acknowledge and thank early childhood development specialist Catherine D. Hughes for her expert insights and guidance. Many thanks also to Lee Langston, an expert with the American Society of Mechanical Engineers, and to researcher Sharon K. Thompson for their invaluable help with this book.